NFL TODAY

THE STORY OF THE
BUFFALO BILLS

NFL TODAY

THE STORY OF THE BUFFALO BILLS

SCOTT CAFFREY

CREATIVE EDUCATION

Cover: Running back Thurman Thomas (top),
quarterback Trent Edwards (bottom)
Page 2: Bills defense, 2007
Pages 4–5: Quarterback Jack Kemp
Pages 6–7: Bills offensive line, 2007

....

Published by Creative Education
P.O. Box 227, Mankato, Minnesota 56002
Creative Education is an imprint of
The Creative Company
www.thecreativecompany.us

Design and production by Blue Design
Design Associate: Sarah Yakawonis
Printed in the United States of America

Photographs by Alamy (culliganphoto, Larry B
Reed), Getty Images (Sylvia Allen/NFL, Doug
Benc, Scott Boehm, Timothy Clary/AFP, Diamond
Images, Focus On Sport, Andy Hayt, George
Long/Sports Illustrated, G. Newman Lowrance,
Al Messerschmidt/NFL, NFL, Hy Peskin/Sports
Illustrated, George Rose, John Ruthroff/AFP, Herb
Scharfman/Sports Imagery, Robert L. Smith/NFL,
Paul Spinelli, Rick Stewart, Rick Stewart/Allsport,
Tony Tomsic/NFL, Charles Aqua Viva/NFL, Herbert
Weitman/NFL Photos, Lou Witt/NFL)

Library of Congress Cataloging-in-Publication Data

Caffrey, Scott.
The story of the Buffalo Bills / by Scott Caffrey.
p. cm. — (NFL today)
Includes index.
ISBN 978-1-58341-748-5
1. Buffalo Bills (Football team)—History—Juvenile
literature. I. Title. II. Series.

GV956.B83C34 2009
796.332'640974797—dc22   2008020705

First Edition
9 8 7 6 5 4 3 2 1

CONTENTS

ON THE SIDELINES

MEET THE BILLS

BUILDING THE BILLS

The city of Buffalo is located in northwestern New York on the shores of Lake Erie. It is a gateway to nearby Niagara Falls and neighboring Ontario, Canada. In 1825, Buffalo boomed with the opening of the Erie Canal, becoming the largest grain-milling center in the United States. Today, it is famous for its powerful winter storms and as the birthplace of Buffalo chicken wings.

Buffalo has also served as a hospitable home for professional football since 1946, when a team called the Buffalo Bisons was formed as part of the All-America Football Conference (AAFC). As is the case with most sports franchises' inaugural seasons, the first-year Bisons struggled that chilly Buffalo fall and winter, going just 3–10–1.

In 1947, the club was renamed the Bills after famous Wild West hunter and entertainer "Buffalo Bill" Cody. That year, the Bills blazed their way to an 8–4–2 record. The next year, behind quarterback George Ratterman and halfback Chet Mutryn, the Bills locked up first place in the league's Eastern Division and beat the Baltimore Colts 28–17 in the Division Championship Game. But Buffalo then got walloped by the Cleveland Browns, 49–7, in the AAFC Championship Game.

In 1949, the Bills dropped to fourth place in their division. That year was also the last for the AAFC. Most of its teams

X Buffalo's growth was due largely to the railroad, grain-milling, and steel-making industries; today, it is known by such nicknames as the "City of Good Neighbors" and "City of Light."

folded, while three of them—the Browns, Colts, and San Francisco 49ers—joined the National Football League (NFL) in 1950. Although Buffalo had more success on the field and in ticket sales than some NFL teams, the franchise's fate was sealed when new owner Jim Breuli decided to fold the team. Some Bills fans transferred their support to other NFL teams, but most chose to be patient.

Those patient fans were rewarded nine years later when Lamar Hunt, a wealthy Texas businessman, gathered seven other millionaires and established the American Football League (AFL) after being denied franchise ownership opportunities in the NFL. One of those millionaires was Ralph Wilson, a minority owner of the NFL's Detroit Lions. Trusted Lions colleagues convinced Wilson that Buffalo should be his only choice because its fans were still hungry for football. After holding a public team-naming contest, Wilson resurrected the Bills name, and Buffalo had its football back in the form of a new AFL franchise.

During those first days, Wilson did just about everything himself, including drafting players. "We had a hat, and we put the names on little pieces of paper and dropped them in ...," he said, explaining the AFL's draft process. "If you wanted a quarterback, you reached in the quarterback hat and

RALPH WILSON

TEAM OWNER
BILLS SEASONS: 1959–PRESENT

Through 2008, Ralph Wilson was the only owner the Buffalo Bills had ever had. Wilson understood early on that in order for the Bills to survive, the AFL had to thrive. So he helped devise the AFL's revenue-sharing plan, which assisted other teams' profitability in the 1960s. Collecting funds from ticket sales and television rights, teams had a pool of money to use in different ways—from player signings to stadium repairs. "I don't think a lot of people realize the amount of money Mr. Wilson pumped into the Bills in those early years in the AFL ...," Bills defensive lineman Tom Day later said. "I don't think Mr. Wilson ever intended to move the Bills to any place other than Buffalo." By 2008, Wilson continued to spearhead the NFL's revenue-sharing plan, and his commitment to his team was rivaled only by his feelings for the Buffalo community. "He cares about the area as well as the football team," general manager Marv Levy said. "And there is nothing that would make him happier than to see the Bills win a Super Bowl."

THESE BILLS LOOK LIKE LIONS

Ralph Wilson was a minority owner of the Detroit Lions for a decade before taking ownership of the Bills in 1959. He looked to Detroit for his first head coach—defensive coordinator Buster Ramsey—and asked the coach to design the team's uniforms. All Ramsey knew was the Lions, so his design basically had the Bills wearing Lions uniforms. "The Bills were a duplicate of the Detroit Lions," trainer Eddie Abramoski said, "starting with the Honolulu blue and silver uniforms." Buffalo uniforms featured blue jerseys with silver trim and pants at home, and white jerseys with blue trim on the road. The helmets also mimicked Detroit's, with a silver base and blue numerals on the sides. When former Boston Patriots coach Lou Saban took over as Buffalo's coach in 1962, he also designed new uniforms that resembled those of his former team. As Bills reporter Jack Horrigan of the *Buffalo Evening News* explained, "Saban decided to 'brighten up' the Bills' new uniforms by adding scarlet and making more use of white than the former silver-blue combination."

drew out a name. That's how I got Richie Lucas." Nicknamed "Riverboat Richie" due to his risk-taking playing style, Lucas was the first player ever drafted by the Bills.

Wilson reached back to his Lions roots to hire defensive coordinator Buster Ramsey as the Bills' first coach in 1960. Ramsey, who was credited with many defensive innovations, including the use of blitzing linebackers, had difficulty building a stable roster. Player turnover during the club's first two seasons (1960 and 1961) seemed to keep the team from jelling. "Everybody who got cut from the NFL, they'd end up in Buffalo," receiver Elbert "Golden Wheels" Dubenion recalled. "You always checked the locker room. 'Practice hard today, there's another wide receiver coming in.' It always kept the pressure on you."

The new Bills struggled at first, but versatile running back Wray Carlton demonstrated a nose for the end zone and helped keep fans interested. But after two straight losing seasons, Ramsey was fired, and player personnel director Lou Saban was promoted to head coach.

Saban's eye for talent helped stabilize the Bills. He took chances on undrafted players such as cornerback Booker Edgerson, journeyman quarterback Jack Kemp, and Canadian Football League running back Carlton "Cookie" Gilchrist. In

X End Mack Yoho (number 82) was part of a tough defense during his four seasons—1960 to 1963—in Buffalo; in 1960, the Bills allowed fewer points than any other AFL team.

1962, Gilchrist became the AFL's first 1,000-yard rusher. His 13 rushing touchdowns also set the all-time AFL record, making Gilchrist an easy choice as the AFL's Most Valuable Player (MVP). "There is no doubt that Cookie was one of the leaders on our team during that era," Carlton recalled years later. "He was one of those punishing running backs."

In 1963, Buffalo started winning, thanks largely to Gilchrist's gritty ball-carrying. In the second-to-last game of that season, he dominated the New York Jets with a pro football-record 243 yards and 5 touchdowns. "There was no stopping Cookie in that game," backup Bills quarterback Daryle Lamonica said. "He was a one-man wrecking crew." Led by Gilchrist's bruising running, Saban's fiery leadership, and kicker and defensive end Mack Yoho's two-way play, Buffalo made the 1963 playoffs. Although they got thumped by the Boston Patriots 26–8, the Bills were starting to roll.

JACK KEMP

QUARTERBACK
BILLS SEASONS: 1962-69
HEIGHT: 6-FOOT-1
WEIGHT: 201 POUNDS

Jack Kemp was involved in one of pro football's first quarterback controversies. After the Buffalo offense stalled in 1964, Kemp was benched in the second-to-last game of the season against Denver. With Buffalo facing a must-win situation against the Boston Patriots the next week to decide the Eastern Division's representative in the AFL Championship Game, Kemp sat next to coach Lou Saban on the plane ride home and spoke up. "I told Saban if he wanted to win he had to play me.... I wasn't putting down [Daryle] Lamonica at all, because he made me a better quarterback, but I told Saban, 'If you start me, I guarantee I'll win this game for you.'" Kemp did start and scored on two quarterback sneaks as Buffalo trumped Boston 24–14. That kind of leadership and ability to back up his words eventually allowed Kemp to cofound the AFL's Players' Association and become its five-time president. It also compelled him to successfully run for a seat in the United States House of Representatives (he served from 1971 to 1989) and to serve as Republican presidential nominee Bob Dole's running mate for vice president in 1996.

[15]

EARLY CHAMPS BECOME ELECTRIC

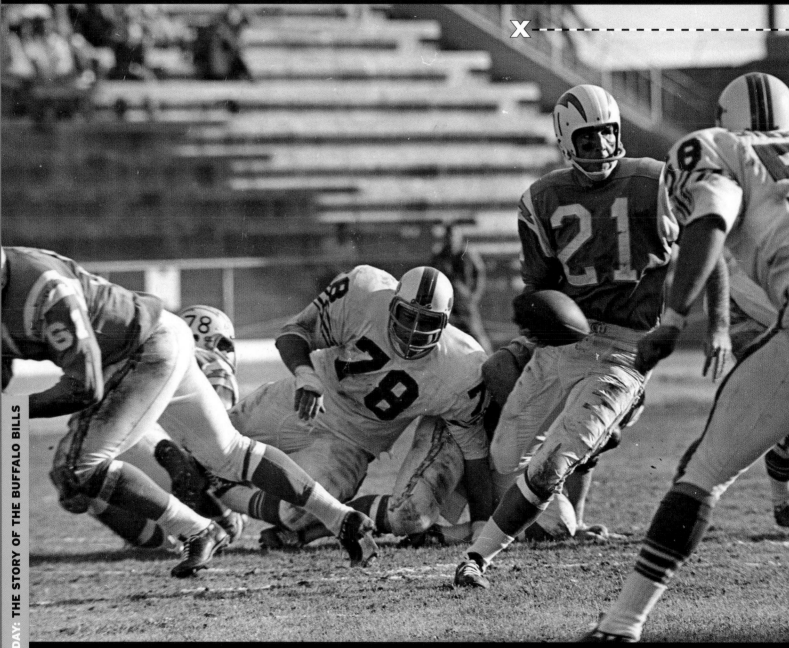

Buffalo started 1964 with nine straight wins behind a defense that was considered the league's best. A rugged offensive line, meanwhile, allowed Kemp to unleash a dangerous air attack with receiver Glenn Bass as the Bills torched opposing defenses.

With a 12–2 record, Buffalo advanced to its first AFL Championship Game to take on the San Diego Chargers. Defensive tackle Tom Sestak led a ferocious line that dismantled the Chargers' passing game, and linebacker Mike Stratton stymied San Diego's running game when he broke Chargers halfback Keith Lincoln's rib on just his third carry. Kemp sealed the 20–7 Bills win with a game-ending quarterback sneak. Afterward, the players felt proud to win for their faithful fans. "The city accepted us and supported us when we were down," said Carlton. "It feels great to give them a championship."

In 1965, the Bills were the AFL team to beat. There were few individual standouts this time as Coach Saban led a balanced, tight-knit team that only got stronger during some close, late-season wins en route to an AFL Championship Game rematch with San Diego. This one was no contest. An early Kemp touchdown pass to Ernie Warlick and a 74-yard punt return touchdown by Butch Byrd gave the Bills an early lead. In the second half, kicker Pete Gogolak booted three field goals, and the Bills defense smothered the Chargers offense in a convincing 23–0 shutout. Then, just a week after the championship repeat, Saban shocked everyone by resigning as coach.

Saban's replacement, Joe Collier, inherited a multitalented team. After opening 1966 with back-to-back losses, Collier patiently led the Bills back to a third straight title game. This time, however, the Kansas City Chiefs were too powerful and handed the Bills a crushing 31–7 loss on New Year's Day.

Buffalo took a big step backward in 1967 with a 4–10 season. Then, during the 1968 preseason, things got worse when Kemp suffered a season-ending knee injury. When the Bills started 0–2 again, Collier was fired. After limping to a 1–12–1 record in what became known in Buffalo as "The Dark Season," the Bills were back where they started—a struggling franchise looking for answers.

The bright side to Buffalo's decline was that the team got the number-one overall pick in the 1969 AFL Draft, which it used on University of Southern California running back Orenthal James (O. J.) Simpson, who had won the Heisman Trophy as college football's best player. Nicknamed "The

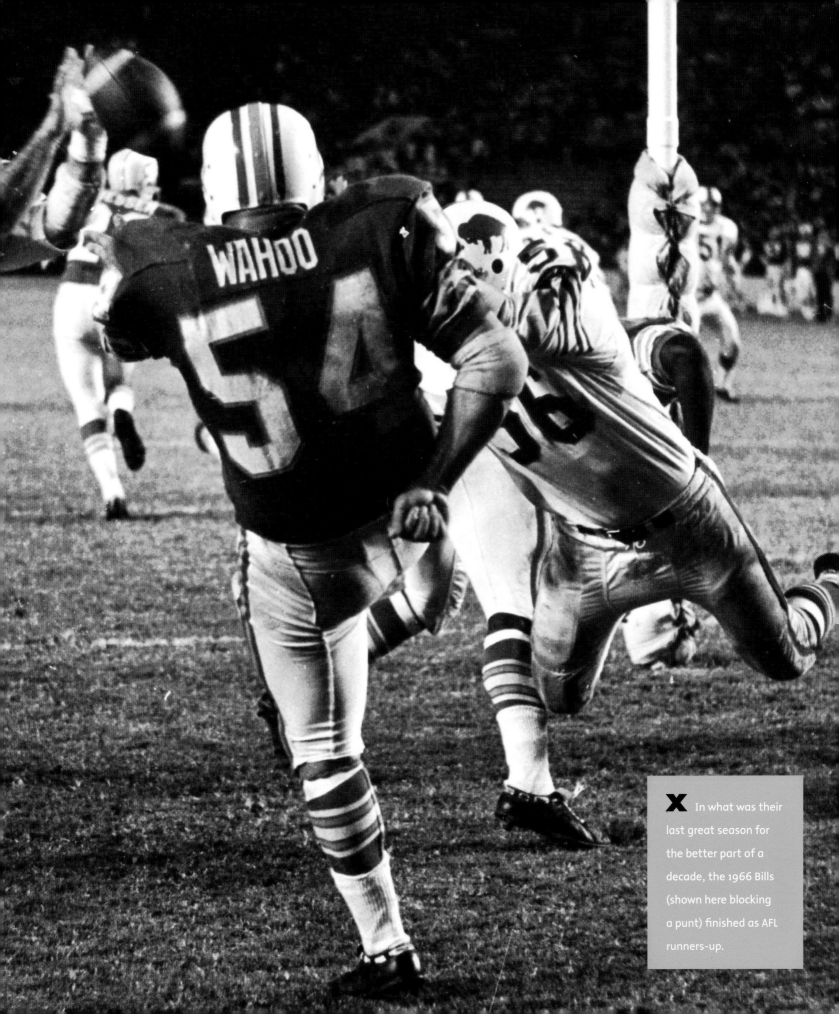

FOOTBALL MEETS SOCCER

Pete Gogolak is responsible for a lot of football "firsts." He was the first placekicker ever drafted by the Bills in 1964, the first "soccer-style" kicker in professional football, and the first player to jump from the AFL to the NFL. "Nobody had ever seen anybody kick the ball this way," Gogolak later recalled. "Before that, [Buffalo] never, ever carried a kicking specialist. Basically, Buffalo took a chance on me." Buffalo took a chance, but quarterback Jack Kemp wasn't about to risk getting his throwing hand kicked, leaving holding duties to backup quarterback Daryle Lamonica. "No one had ever held for a soccer-style kicker, but he knew exactly how he wanted the ball ...," Lamonica said. "His ball just exploded and got great height. Nobody could jump up and block it. He was a real asset." Gogolak helped the Bills win back-to-back AFL championships over the San Diego Chargers in 1964 and 1965. The second championship was Gogolak's finale with the Bills. Four months later, he became the first AFL player to cross over to the NFL, joining the New York Giants.

Juice," Simpson was barely used by new coach John Rauch,

who preferred to move the ball by air rather than by ground.

That unbalanced offense contributed to a meager 4–10

record. Then, as the AFL and NFL merged in 1970, things got

worse for Buffalo, as it dropped to a 3–10–1 record.

After Buffalo hit rock bottom again in 1971 with just one

win, a frustrated Simpson considered quitting. But then, like

the cavalry, Lou Saban returned as head coach and made

plans to revive the team by running the ball—and running it

X From 1960 to
1972, the Bills played
their home games in
Buffalo's War Memorial
Stadium, known to
local sports fans as
"The Rockpile."

X A track star in college, O. J. Simpson used his long-striding rushing style to post the longest runs in the NFL in 1972, 1973, and 1975 (94, 80, and 88 yards, respectively).

some more. After handing the ball to Simpson during practice, the coach said to his offensive linemen, "There's your meal ticket. Go block for him." And block they did as Simpson ran for 1,251 yards in 1972. Buffalo's offensive line—consisting of center Bruce Jarvis, guards Reggie McKenzie and Joe DeLamielleure, and tackles Donnie Green and Dave Foley—grew so skilled at opening holes that they became known as the "Electric Company" because they "turned on The Juice."

When players reported to training camp in the summer of 1973, McKenzie was so confident of the team's success that he pulled Simpson aside and made a bold prediction. "Juice, this season you are going to accomplish something that no other running back has ever done," he said. "You're gonna rush for two grand."

Simpson would have been happy just to break his idol Jim Brown's NFL record of 1,863 rushing yards. After The Juice cracked a rib in practice, the team didn't allow him to play in any preseason games. The time spent resting paid off, as he opened the season by gaining a then NFL-record 250 yards in a 31–13 win over the New England Patriots.

Simpson gained more than 100 yards in each of his next 4 games, and the only teams to keep him under 100 during the rest of the season were the Miami Dolphins (55 yards), New Orleans Saints (79), and Cincinnati Bengals (99). "O. J. was a

JOE DeLAMIELLEURE

GUARD
BILLS SEASONS: 1973-79, 1985
HEIGHT: 6-FOOT-3
WEIGHT: 254 POUNDS

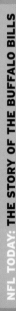

After being selected in the first round of the 1973 NFL Draft by the Bills, Joe DeLamielleure immediately commanded respect. "Mr. Wilson told me that to this day I am the only player he personally called to inform that I had been drafted by Buffalo," DeLamielleure later wrote in his autobiography. An immediate starter his rookie season, "Joe D" went on to win All-Rookie honors and to become one of the team's greatest offensive linemen. Known for his brilliant run blocking, the swift-pulling DeLamielleure was also a deft pass blocker. Durable and dependable, he played in 185 consecutive games in 13 seasons with the Bills and the Cleveland Browns. "As I matured as a player, I realized that it took more brains than brawn to keep playing," he said. "I probably went downhill physically during my later years, but I played better because I got smarter. [Oakland Raiders linebacker] Ted Hendricks told me to 'stay low, keep your feet moving, and avoid any pileups.' And over time I added one more tip—play until the whistle blows." DeLamielleure left Buffalo in 1979 but returned six years later to finish his career there.

thing of beauty to watch," said Bills cornerback Robert James. "He did things that nobody had seen before on a football field." Finally, on December 16, during a snowy afternoon game against the New York Jets, Simpson surpassed the expectations of everyone but McKenzie by rushing for 200 yards to become the first NFL running back to break the 2,000-yard barrier, finishing with 2,003.

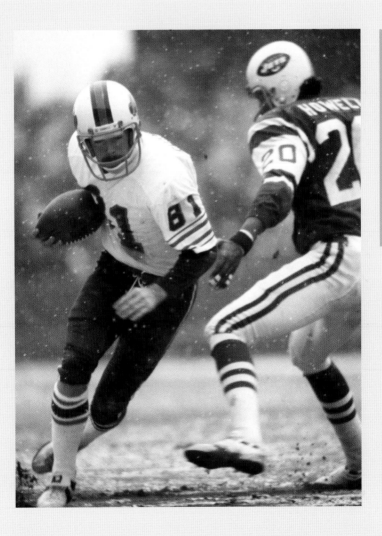

X Although O. J. Simpson dominated Buffalo's headlines in the '70s, receiver Bob Chandler caught 370 passes to help drive the Bills' passing attack from 1971 to 1979.

x--------

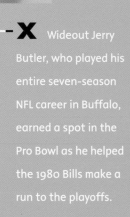

The Bills enjoyed some productive seasons in the early 1970s but never got back to the postseason. Finally, a 2–12 record in 1976 led to Saban's second departure. Team owner Ralph Wilson then became the envy of the league when he hired Los Angeles Rams coach Chuck Knox. Nicknamed "Ground Chuck" due to his love of a run-based offense and powerful defense, Knox had taken his Rams to five consecutive divisional titles. Shortly after he arrived in Buffalo, Knox traded the aging and injury-prone Simpson to the 49ers for five draft picks over three years, which he used to select players such as wide receiver Jerry Butler and scrappy linebacker Jim Haslett. By 1980, Knox had laid the foundation for a new era of hope in Buffalo.

By then, Buffalo's rushing attack was led by Joe Cribbs. Many experts thought that the 5-foot-11 and 190-pound Cribbs was too small to be an effective running back. But he quickly proved them wrong, rushing for more than 1,000 yards in 3 of his first 4 seasons. "What they didn't measure on Joe was his toughness," said nose tackle Fred

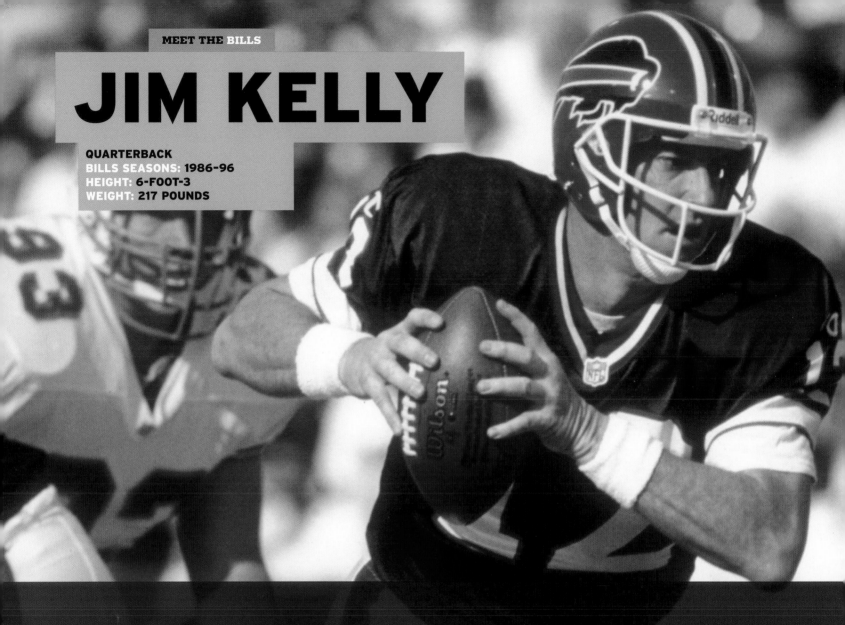

JIM KELLY

QUARTERBACK
BILLS SEASONS: 1986-96
HEIGHT: 6-FOOT-3
WEIGHT: 217 POUNDS

It was sometimes said that Jim Kelly was "a quarterback with a linebacker's mentality." There are many examples of his toughness. But one home game in 1990 against the Arizona Cardinals symbolized it best. After being hit in the jaw by blitzing Arizona safety Leonard Smith, Kelly went down and fumbled the ball. A Cardinals defensive lineman scooped it up and ran with it. After the lineman finally was brought down, the referees separated players from the pile. There, at the bottom of the pile, was Kelly, still tussling with the bigger lineman for the ball. He lost the ball but gained even more respect from his teammates. "Like Babe Ruth was to the [New York] Yankees and Michael Jordan was to the [Chicago] Bulls, Jim Kelly is to the Bills," Bills receiver Steve Tasker once wrote. "He taught us how to win and, in the process, saved the franchise." Kelly was so respected that coach Marv Levy and offensive coordinator Ted Marchibroda treated the Hall-of-Famer like an on-field coach. They valued his opinion about personnel, play calls, and team decisions as much as that of any team executive.

[28]

Smerlas. "Pound for pound, Joe was the toughest guy in the league." Thanks largely to Cribbs and a rugged defense that featured linebackers Isiah Robertson and Phil Villapiano, the Bills made the playoffs in 1980 and 1981. But they were knocked out each time, first by the Chargers, then by the Cincinnati Bengals.

Then, just as the Bills were improving, the momentum was lost in 1982 with the departure of both Cribbs and Knox and a players' strike that shortened the season. The losses then continued to mount in three straight losing seasons. "We were so bad," Smerlas joked, "the only thing that showed up at Rich Stadium on Sundays were the snowflakes."

Midway through a horrid 1986 season, Wilson hired a new coach in Marv Levy, whose optimistic and enthusiastic attitude was a breath of fresh air for the downtrodden Bills. His first key decision was to sign Houston Oilers reserve receiver Steve Tasker. What seemed like an afterthought at the time proved to be one of his smartest moves—the diminutive, 5-foot-9 Tasker epitomized Levy's hard-working, team-first philosophy. "When we were down, Marv showed us the way up," Tasker said. And over the next two seasons, Levy showed the Bills the way to two straight American Football Conference (AFC) East Division titles.

During these years, the Bills were built around four special players: defensive end Bruce Smith, receiver Andre Reed, quarterback Jim Kelly, and running back Thurman Thomas. Although Smith and Reed were both drafted in 1985, they came from very different backgrounds. Smith was the top overall pick in the NFL Draft after emerging as a major college star at Virginia Tech. Reed was a little-known, fourth-round talent from Kutztown University in Pennsylvania.

Kelly originally spurned the Bills after they drafted him in 1983 and played for the Houston Gamblers in the short-lived United States Football League (USFL). When the USFL disbanded after the 1985 season, Kelly said publicly that he would rather play for a more glamorous team in a warmer climate than Buffalo. Although he finally suited up for Buffalo in 1986, the Bills suffered back-to-back losing seasons, and fans were very down on him. Eventually, though, Kelly would come to appreciate Buffalo, and his toughness, smarts, and gamesmanship would win the fans over.

Thomas represented the final piece of the puzzle when he arrived in 1988. A multitalented athlete, Thomas was a superb runner and receiver who did all the little things that helped the Bills win. His blocking skills set him apart from the competition, and he is still widely considered to have been one

THE BUFFALO CURSE

"The Buffalo Curse" is a mythical explanation for Buffalo's professional sports teams' inability to win league championships. After winning two AFL championships in the mid-1960s, the Bills have never won the Super Bowl. Likewise, the Sabres of the National Hockey League have never won a Stanley Cup, despite several close calls. The alleged curse really seemed to take hold in 1990 after kicker Scott Norwood's failed last-second field goal attempt handed the Giants a Super Bowl XXV victory. The Bills lost three more Super Bowls after that (after the 1991, 1992, and 1993 seasons). Then, between 1993 and 2008, the Bills won only one playoff game. There are a couple of notable curse theories. One legend explains that Seneca Indian chief Red Jacket once put a curse on the entire city. Another notes the assassination of former president William McKinley at Buffalo's Pan American Exposition in 1901. A January 2008 chant ceremony led by a paranormalist named Mason C. Winfield III claimed to have lifted the curse for good. "Put off your aches, your pains, your ills ...," the chant went. "God bless our Sabres and our Bills."

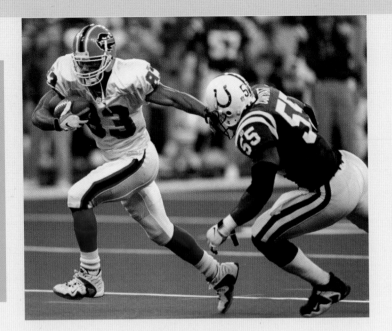

X Although not as fast or flashy as some star receivers of the '90s, Andre Reed was as durable and steady as they come, playing in 234 career games and making 7 consecutive Pro Bowls.

of the best backs in NFL history at stopping blitzing defenders.

With this talent at their disposal, Levy and offensive coordinator Ted Marchibroda built the "K-Gun" offense. In it, Kelly lined up in the shotgun formation (several yards behind the center), from which he could either hand off to Thomas or fire passes downfield to Reed. The offense also often ran plays without a huddle, which tired out opposing defenses. "Playing against the Bills is like getting caught in a hurricane," said Los Angeles Raiders defensive end Howie Long. "They are relentless." During the 1989 off-season, Kelly lobbied Coach Levy to install the no-huddle offense full-time, and Buffalo's offense really went wild.

On defense, meanwhile, Smith was tireless in his pursuit of opposing quarterbacks, posting 10 or more sacks per season in 12 of his 15 years in Buffalo. With linebackers Darryl Talley and Cornelius Bennett also wreaking havoc, the Bills were ready to rule the AFC.

Known for his friendly, soft-spoken personality off the field, Bruce Smith turned into a quarterback-hunting terror when he lined up on Sundays. **X**

SUPER BOWL
HEARTACHE

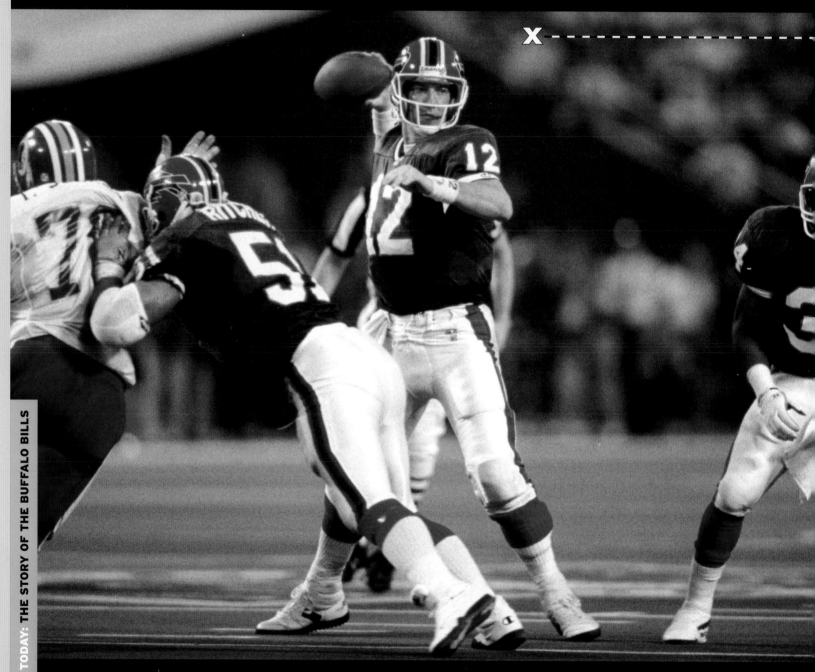

X Their running
game shut down, the
Bills went to the air
in Super Bowl XXVI
against the Redskins,
with Jim Kelly tossing
a Super Bowl-record
58 passes in the
losing effort.

From 1990 to 1993, Buffalo set an NFL record by advancing to four consecutive Super Bowls. In 1990, the Bills nearly doubled the combined scoring output of their opponents (428–263) and then romped over teams in the playoffs, including a 51–3 destruction of the Raiders in the AFC Championship Game.

But in Super Bowl XXV against the New York Giants, the Giants' offense thwarted Buffalo's momentum by holding the ball for almost twice the amount of time that Buffalo did. With the Giants leading 20–19 and just 4 seconds left on the clock, Bills kicker Scott Norwood lined up for a 47-yard field goal that would have captured the Bills' first NFL championship. Instead, it sailed wide right. "That ball slid by that upright by about a foot," Kelly said sadly. "We were a foot away from being champions."

In 1991, Buffalo's offense was even better. Kelly passed for 3,844 yards and 33 touchdowns. And although Thomas accounted for more than 2,000 total yards, he inexplicably disappeared in Super Bowl XXVI against the Washington

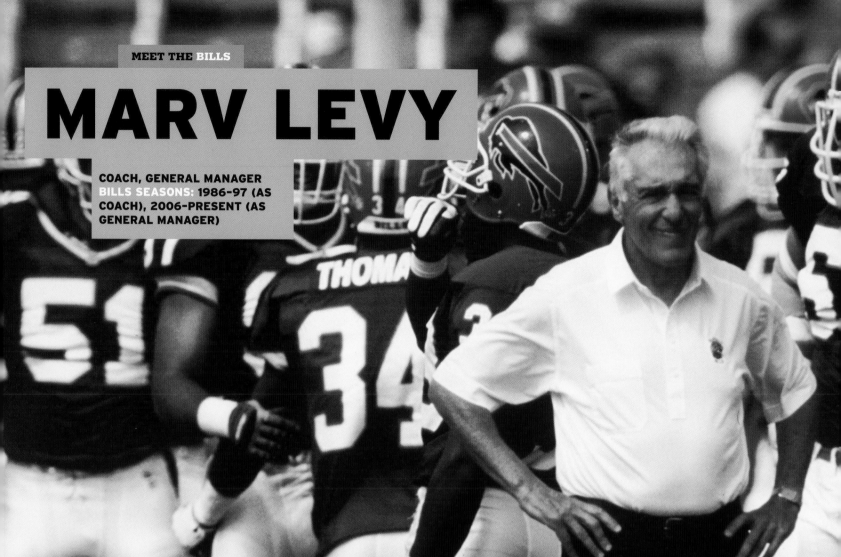

MARV LEVY

COACH, GENERAL MANAGER
BILLS SEASONS: 1986-97 (AS COACH), 2006-PRESENT (AS GENERAL MANAGER)

Harvard-educated Marv Levy was not just a great coach—he was also a great teacher. His locker-room speeches became legendary, often featuring quotes from famous leaders such as Winston Churchill and Franklin Delano Roosevelt, and he sometimes used World War II analogies to drive his points home. But often, it wasn't about the words he used. Levy started his pro career as a special-teams coach with the Washington Redskins. So it wasn't unusual that, two weeks after Steve Tasker signed with the Bills in 1986, Levy spent 45 minutes after practice, in the snow, teaching Tasker how to block punts. "He was in his early 60s at the time, but that didn't stop him from getting down in a stance and showing me how to take the path off the corner," Tasker wrote. "He was one of the first coaches to understand that special teams accounted for a third of the plays in a football game, so you had better be good at it." That kind of dedication gave Levy and the Bills a 123–78 record in 12 seasons (a .612 winning percentage), 8 playoff appearances, and an NFL-record four straight Super Bowl berths.

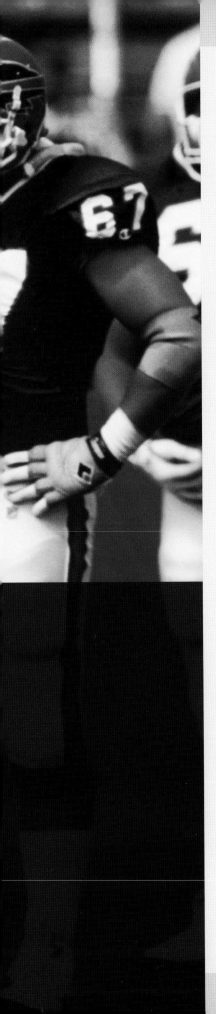

Redskins. After misplacing his helmet and missing the game's opening series, Thomas fizzled with just 13 rushing yards. Buffalo again came up short, this time 37–24.

Still, in 1992, Buffalo remained the AFC's top squad. After backup quarterback Frank Reich directed a monumental 41–38 comeback win over the Houston Oilers in the first round of the playoffs, Buffalo cruised through the next two rounds. But the Bills were once again outmatched in the Super Bowl, this time losing 52–17 to the Dallas Cowboys.

The next year's Super Bowl was a highly anticipated rematch with Dallas. After kicker Steve Christie boomed a Super Bowl-record 54-yard field goal in the first quarter, the

X Steve Christie's record-setting 54-yard field goal in Super Bowl XXVIII was one of the last great highlights of the Bills' famous Super Bowl run.

X Eric Moulds emerged as a star in 1998, leading the AFC in receiving yards (1,368) during the regular season, then posting a whopping 240 more in a playoff game after the season.

Bills marched to a 13–6 halftime lead. But they never scored another point, and Dallas pulled away to win 30–13. Despite the pain of four straight Super Bowl losses, Wilson remained proud. "No matter what the scoreboard said," he said, "this team was a champion in my heart."

After 1994, even excellent efforts from such players as linebacker Bryce Paup couldn't get the Bills back to the Super Bowl. Kelly retired in 1996 after a demoralizing 30–27 playoff loss to the Jacksonville Jaguars. Levy left after a 6–10 season in 1997, and eventually Thomas, Smith, and Reed moved on. "We were blessed to have a core of guys who gave

THE BACKUP'S COMEBACK

In 1984, quarterback Frank Reich was responsible for what was then the biggest comeback in the history of college football. As the backup to Stan Gelbaugh at the University of Maryland, Reich stepped in and led the Terrapins back from a first-half deficit of 31–0 to a 42–40 victory over the previously unbeaten University of Miami. So when the Bills called on Reich in a 1992 playoff game against the Houston Oilers in place of an injured Jim Kelly, he already had some come-from-behind mojo working in his favor. Consistently connecting with wide receiver Andre Reed, Reich led the Bills back from a 35–3 deficit to a 41–38 victory. Kicker Steve Christie booted the winning field goal in overtime to cap the largest comeback in NFL history. Reich also started the next week in a playoff matchup in Pittsburgh against the Steelers, leading Buffalo to a 24–3 win. "The guys on this team were so encouraging," Reich said. "They kept me up when it could have been real easy to get down."

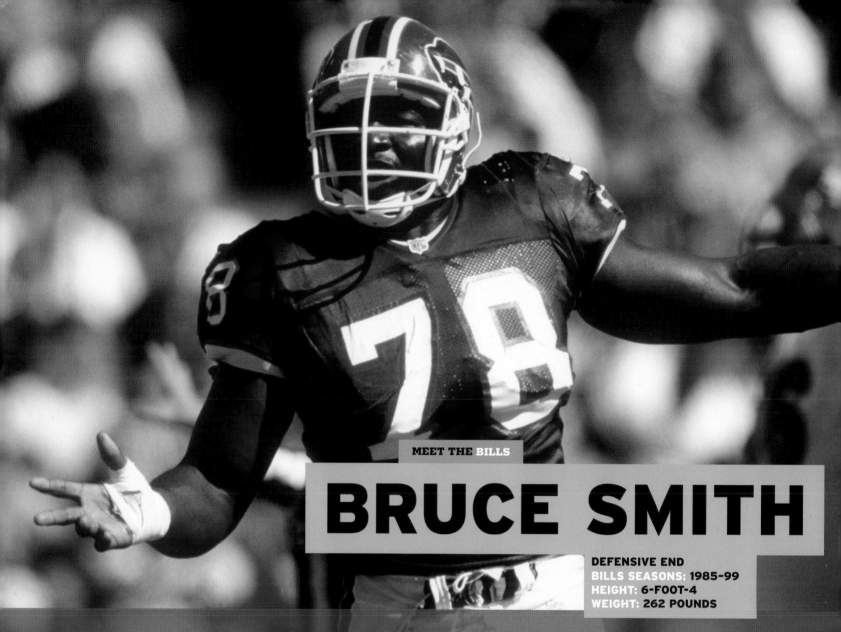

BRUCE SMITH

DEFENSIVE END
BILLS SEASONS: 1985-99
HEIGHT: 6-FOOT-4
WEIGHT: 262 POUNDS

After winning the Outland Trophy as America's top college lineman, Bruce Smith became the first overall pick of the 1985 NFL Draft. During his 15-year career with Buffalo, the "Sack Man" became one of the greatest NFL defensive players ever. An exceptionally quick and powerful pass rusher, Smith was also a superb run-stuffer, often forcing opposing offenses to completely avoid his side. In 1990, Smith tallied a career-high 19 sacks and won the first of 2 NFL Defensive Player of the Year awards (the other coming in 1996). Smith set a league record by notching at least 10 sacks in 13 seasons. When Buffalo cut him in 1999 to save money in the new salary cap era (which limited teams' payrolls to create a balanced playing field), Smith was heavy-hearted. "I wish I had the opportunity to play in front of our fans one more time, knowing that it was my last time," Smith said. "After 15 years in one place, the fans deserved better. I never got a chance to say goodbye." He ended his career with the Washington Redskins in 2003 as the NFL's all-time sack leader (200).

it everything they had, every Sunday," Levy said. "It was an honor to lead such men."

Levy's replacement, Wade Phillips, built a winner in 1998 (10–6) and 1999 (11–5) with quarterback Doug Flutie and sure-handed receiver Eric Moulds, and Buffalo made the playoffs as a Wild Card both years. The 1999 playoff game against the Tennessee Titans was a heartbreaker. Buffalo was just 16 seconds away from a 16–15 victory when it kicked off to Tennessee. A Titans blocker handed the ball to tight end Frank Wycheck, who fired a long, cross-field lateral to receiver Kevin Dyson. Dyson then sprinted 75 yards for the miraculous, winning score. "My heart sank when I saw that guy cross the goal line," said Bills defensive end Phil Hansen. "I thought the game was in the bag." After Buffalo fell to 8–8 in 2000, Phillips was fired.

New coach Gregg Williams oversaw a 3–13 season in 2001. Seeking a boost, Buffalo traded with the New England Patriots for star quarterback Drew Bledsoe. With Bledsoe orchestrating the offense and running back Travis Henry galloping for 1,438 yards, the Bills climbed back to 8–8 in 2002. But despite a talented defense led by hard-hitting linebacker Takeo Spikes, Buffalo continued its up-and-down trend, dropping to 6–10 the next season.

X A two-time Pro-Bowler and defensive leader, linebacker Takeo Spikes was a tackling machine with a nose for the ball; in 2004, he picked off five passes, returning two for touchdowns.

In 2006, after two more mediocre seasons in Buffalo, Marv Levy returned to the team as general manager, and new coach Dick Jauron led Buffalo to back-to-back 7–9 records. Although the Bills remained outside the AFC playoff picture, fans found reasons for optimism as young quarterback Trent Edwards led the team to a surprising 4–0 start in 2008. The offense, led by swift receiver Lee Evans and flashy halfback Marshawn Lynch, showed some explosiveness, while young linebacker Paul Posluszny and defensive end Aaron Schobel looked to resurrect Buffalo's tradition of a stout defense.

DEDICATION TO FOOTBALL'S FUTURE

The Buffalo Bills have long maintained a commitment to their youngest fans. And on November 12, 2004, they made history by becoming the first NFL franchise to build a whole facility dedicated to youth football on the grounds of the team's headquarters. "We are very committed in our organization to do things to give back to our community, and one of our primary initiatives is youth football," team president and general manager Tom Donahoe said. The Buffalo Bills Youth Football Field was built just behind Ralph Wilson Stadium, where the Bills' outdoor practice field used to be. The regulation-size field had a full-sized scoreboard in the end zone and numerous temporary bleachers for fans. The field was centrally located and therefore easily accessed by the 300 youth football teams throughout the large western New York, Niagara Falls, and Erie County area. "This is the future of the National Football League," Bills cornerback Troy Vincent said at the ribbon-cutting ceremony. "These programs are really important for us in both teaching the game and teaching kids how to lead a successful life."

X Due to Buffalo's extra-snowy location, many late-season Bills games can turn into old-fashioned slugfests in wintry, slippery conditions.

STAMPEDING INTO TORONTO

In his 2007 state of the league address, NFL commissioner Roger Goodell confirmed that plans for the Buffalo Bills to play five regular-season games and three preseason games in Toronto over the following five years were finalized. The "Toronto Initiative" was to consist of one regular-season game at the Rogers Centre in downtown Toronto each year of the five-year pact, and one preseason game there every other year. Goodell, a western New York native, was impressed by the Bills' proposal. "I think it was done very thoughtfully," he said. "I think it was done to help regionalize the team on an even broader scale than they have. They have regionalized throughout western New York, and that's helped the team be more successful from a business standpoint and market themselves more effectively. They have a tremendous amount of interest north into Canada and the Hamilton-Toronto area." Although the league had already played games in Mexico and London by then, the Bills were set to blaze a trail—becoming the first NFL team to play at least one annual "home" game outside the U.S.

For more than 40 years, the Buffalo Bills have provided fans in northwestern New York with autumn excitement. From their championship days in the AFL to their great run of the early '90s, Buffalo has earned the adulation of one of the most loyal fan bases in the NFL. And with today's Bills on the rise, it may not be long before a Lombardi Trophy finally makes its way to Buffalo.

X Halfback Marshawn Lynch opened eyes around the NFL as a rookie in 2007, scampering for 1,115 rushing yards for the improving Bills.

INDEX